Celebratin Croissants

40 Fabulous Fillings for National Croissant Day - Ideal for a Bistro Breakfast or Light Lunch

BY

Daniel Humphreys

License Notes

Table of Contents

Introduction

On January 30th each year National Croissant Day pays homage to this delicious, crescent-shaped, little pastry.

Here are some fun and historical facts about this buttery puff pastry we all know and love today.

The first croissant, or Kipfel as it was known by, originated in Austria at the end of the 17th century, when in 1683 the Austrians were victorious against the Turks. Its crescent design modeled after the crescent shape on Turkey's flag.

When Austrian artillery officer, August Zang, opened his Viennese style bakery in Paris, he is said to have brought the croissant recipe with him.

In 1920 the pastry became France's national product.

Initially starting out as luxury baked goods, by the end of the 19th century, the croissant became the choice of the middle classes.

Some say that when Marie Antoinette uttered the immortal words 'let them eat cake,' she was referring to croissants!

So, whether you simply like your croissants warm, slathered with jam or filled with curried chicken, pop into your local bakery or even try making your own at home.

Celebrating Croissants will not only show you how to make basic, buttery croissants from scratch but also lots of sweet and savory fabulous fillings, too.

The Basics

Almond Croissants

Making your own croissants is not as difficult as you may think. With this classic almond recipe, you can make the ultimate stand-alone snack, or split open and pack with your favorite fillings.

Servings: 2

Prep Time: 15mins

Cooking Time: 20mins

Total Time: 40mins

Ingredients:

- cup almond meal
- cup sugar
- tsp vanilla extract
- 4 tbsp. butter (softened, room temperature)
- 1 large organic egg
- 2 croissants* (split in half)
- Powdered sugar
- Toasted almonds (sliced)

Directions:

1. Preheat the main oven to 350 degrees F. Take a baking sheet and line it with parchment paper and prepare your ingredients.

2. First, make the filling by combining the almond meal with the sugar, vanilla extract, softened butter, and egg in a blender or food processor, and blend until a creamy consistency.

3. Next, fill the croissants: Lay the bottom halves of the 2 croissants onto the baking sheet. Split the filling between them, evenly spreading the mixture. Place the tops on each of the croissants to form a sandwich.

4. Bake the croissant sandwiches in the oven until the filling is no longer gooey, but set, this will take around 15-20 minutes.

5. Remove from the oven and allow to rest for 5 minutes.

6. As soon as the croissants are sufficiently cool enough to handle add 2-3 spoonfuls of the powdered sugar into a mesh sieve and sift over the croissants.

7. Scatter the croissants with toasted almonds and serve warm.

*Preferably one day old.

Classic Croissants

Follow our step-by-step recipe to make a classic baked croissant worthy of your favorite bakery or pastry shop.

Servings: 12-14

Prep Time: 1hour 15mins

Cooking Time: 20mins

Total Time: 12hours 35mins

Ingredients:

- 17ounces premium white flour + additional for dusting and work surface
- 1ounces sugar
- 1tsp table salt
- 1cups cold water
- 2 (ounce) sachets dried yeast (fast auctioned)
- Oil (to grease)
- 1cups butter (room temperature)
- 1 large egg (beaten)

Directions:

1. Add the white flour along with the sugar, and salt in a large bowl.

2. In a jug, add 1 cups of cold water. Next, add the dried yeast, stirring to combine.

3. Form a well shape in the middle of the flour mixture and slowly add the yeast liquid. Mix and knead on a clean surface for several minutes. Shape the dough into a round ball and place in a bowl lightly greased with oil, cover the bowl and allow to chill for a minimum of 2 hours.

4. Place the butter in between two sheets of parchment paper and with a rolling pin, lightly bash the butter and roll into a rectangular shape of approximately 8x6". Leave the butter, wrapped in parchment and refrigerate.

5. Once the dough is sufficiently chilled, place it on a lightly floured, clean work surface and roll out into a rectangular shape of around 16x8". Transfer the slab of butter, unwrapped, in the middle of the dough, in order to cover the middle third.

6. Fold one side of the chilled dough upwards and halfway over the butter.

7. Repeating the same method, fold the other side of the dough; the two edges need to meet each other in the middle of the butter, also known as a 'book' fold.

8. Fold the dough over, in half, in order that the point where the dough ends meet form a seam. Wrap in plastic kitchen wrap and transfer to the refrigerator to chill for 30-40 minutes.

9. Repeat, the process of rolling, folding, followed by chilling another two times, using exactly the same method. Do not add additional butter. Wrap in plastic kitchen wrap and chill, for several hours or preferably overnight.

10. The following day, using a rolling pin, roll the dough out onto a lightly floured work surface in a large rectangular shape, measuring approximately 24"x12" and using a pizza cutter or sharp kitchen knife, trim and neaten the edges.

11. Cut the dough into 2 equal portions, lengthwise to form 2 strips, and then cut each strip into 6 triangular shapes with 2 equal sides.

12. Take each of the 6 triangles and gently pull the 2 corners at the triangle's base to widen and stretch.

13. Beginning at the triangle's base, gently roll into a crescent shape, taking care not to crush.

14. Continue to roll, while ensuring that the tip of each of the 6 triangles ends up are neatly tucked under the croissant, this will help it to hold in position.

15. Bend the ends of each croissant inwards, and transfer to 1 or 2 parchment lined baking trays. Cover with lightly greased or oiled plastic wrap and set to one side to rise, until twice the size, or for a minimum of 2 hours.

16. Preheat the main oven to 400 degrees F.

17. In a small bowl, add the beaten egg together with a pinch of salt, mix to combine and brush generously over the croissants to glaze.

18. Bake in the oven for 15-20 minutes, or until golden and risen.

Allow to cool on baking racks.

Homemade Chocolate Croissants

Everyone loves chocolate croissants, so why not learn how to make your own flakey, buttery treats?

Servings: 6-8

Prep Time: 30mins

Cooking Time: 15mins

Total Time: 8hours 45mins

Ingredients

- cup whole milk (warm)
- 1cups strong bread flour + extra for work surface
- tsp salt
- 4 tbsp. sugar
- 2 tsp dry yeast
- 11 tbsp. butter (frozen)
- 4 ounces dark (72%) chocolate chips
- 1 egg yolk beaten + 1 tbsp. milk (for glazing)

Directions:

1. In a small pan, warm the milk to body temperature.

2. In a mixing bowl, add the bread flour to the salt, sugar, and dry yeast, whisking to combine.

3. Using a metal grater, grate the frozen butter directly into the flour, until you achieve pea-size pieces.

4. Pour in the tepid milk and combine to form dough; you can do this using a spoon.

5. Turn this dough out onto a lightly floured, clean work surface and press together to form a square. Wrap the soft dough in plastic wrap and transfer to the refrigerator for 1hours.

6. Lightly dust your work surface and rolling pin with flour.

7. Roll the dough out into a rectangular shape of approximately 15x10".

8. Next, fold the shorter sides of the dough into the center.

9. By one quarter turn, rotate the dough, rolling out to lengthen and folding the shorter ends towards the center.

10. Flip the dough over so that the seams are underneath.

11. Roll out once more while repeating the folding steps another two times.

12. The dough will be more elastic as you roll and fold.

13. During this process should the butter become too soft, cover the dough and place it in the freezer to firm a little, before continuing to roll and fold.

14. The dough needs to be a small rectangular shape.

15. Wrap the dough twice with plastic wrap and transfer to the refrigerator, overnight.

16. Roll your dough out to a rectangle which is approximately three times longer than it is wide and at least 1?" thick. Using a pastry scraper trim the pastry edges.

17. Cut the dough into triangular shapes of approximately 12" in length and 3" at the base.

18. Using a sharp knife, cut a small slit in the middle of each triangle base.

19. Carefully, stretch the corners along with the tip, adding the chocolate chips to the wide end and then loosely roll up the dough. Placing tip side facing down, on a large baking tray lined with parchment paper.

20. Repeat the process with the remaining dough, and space the croissants 2-3" apart from one another on the baking tray.

21. Loosely cover the dough with lightly greased plastic wrap, allow the croissants to rise for around 2-3 hours at room temperature.

22. Preheat the main oven to 450 degrees F.

23. Lightly brush each croissant with the egg wash and bake in the oven for 10 minutes.

24. Turn the temperature down to 375 degrees F and bake in the oven for another 5-6 minutes, or until golden and browned.

25. Cool on a wire baking rack and serve.

Mini Vegan Croissants

Dairy free vegan croissants that need a lot of patience but are well worth the baking effort so why not double up and make a big batch?

Servings: 12

Prep Time: 25mins

Cooking Time: 20mins

Total Time: 50mins

Ingredients

Dough:

- 2cups bread flour
- 1 tsp salt
- 2 tbsp. + 2 tsp sugar
- 1 tsp active dry yeast
- cup + 2 tsp water
- 1tbsp. dairy-free stick margarine (melted)
- Oil (for greasing)
- Butter Block:
- 9 tbsp. dairy-free, stick margarine (frozen)

Directions:

1. First, make the dough. Add the flour, salt, sugar, and dry yeast in a mixing bowl. Mix until well combined.

2. Add the water along with the melted margarine and thoroughly stir to combine. Knead, until a smooth dough is formed and allow to chill in the refrigerator for 25-35 minutes.

3. Roll the dough out onto a clean, lightly floured work surface, and using your hands, knead for 12-15 minutes, or until the dough is elastic yet smooth. Transfer the dough to a bowl that is lightly greased, and cover totally with kitchen wrap. Allow to rest in the fridge for half an hour.

4. In the meantime, and while the dough is chilling prepare the butter block.

5. First, cut the margarine into sizeable and easy to handle chunks, and arrange next to one another on a sheet of parchment.

6. Sandwich the margarine between another sheet of parchment and with a wooden rolling pin, hit it hard. You are aiming to flatten it to around no more than ?" thick while attempting to keep the sides even and a rectangular shape. Transfer to the refrigerator to chill for half an hour.

7. Preheat the main oven to 415 degrees F.

8. Once sufficiently chilled, roll the dough out into a rectangular shape around the same size as your butter block.

9. Arrange the butter block in the middle and diagonal rather than parallel to the sides. Enclose the butter block as you would an envelope, by bringing the corners to meet in the middle.

10. Roll out carefully to a ?" thickness, folding the shorter sides in by thirds. Return the dough to the refrigerator and chill for 20 minutes. It is vital that the dough is as cool as possible before it is put in the oven.

11. Once again, roll out the dough into a rectangular shape, and fold into thirds once again. Chill and repeat the process once again. Chill the dough for a further 25 minutes before shaping the dough.

12. Next, to shape the mini croissants, roll the dough into a rectangular shape as before, but using a very sharp knife cut the dough in half lengthwise and then into equal triangles.

13. Roll each of the triangles up, starting at their widest side and place each mini croissant on a piece of parchment.

14. As soon as all of the croissants are rolled and cut, allow them to rise at room temperature for around 1 hour and 15mins, or until nearly doubled in size.

15. Once risen, transfer the mini croissants to a preheated oven at 415 degrees F.

16. Close the oven door and immediately turn the heat down to 350 degrees F.

17. After 15 minutes have gone by and not before, check the croissants, they should be golden, and if they aren't, return to the oven for 5-10 minutes.

18. Allow to cool and serve.

Spelt Croissants

Thisspelt croissant recipe is a challenge, but it allows you to make perfect patisserie treats in your own kitchen with these all butter traditional croissants.

Servings: 16

Prep Time: 1hour

Cooking Time: 25mins

Total Time: 16hours 25mins

Ingredients:

- 1 cup whole milk (warm)
- 1ounces brown sugar
- 1 ounce fresh yeast
- 10ounces whole grain spelt flour + extra for work surface
- 2 tsp table salt
- 1ounces unsalted butter (cold)
- 1 medium egg

Directions:

1. In the bowl of an electric stand mixer, stir the whole milk together with the brown sugar, followed by the yeast and allow to stand for 4-6 minutes, or until foamy. Add the flour along with the salt and on low speed, while using your mixer's dough hook, mix for another 4-6 minutes until soft and smooth.

2. Place the dough on a clean countertop and using clean hands, knead for a couple of minutes, gradually adding additional flour, to achieve slightly sticky but soft dough. Next, using a sheet of plastic wrap, cover the dough and allow to chill for 60 minutes.

3. Arrange the butter in between 2 sheets of plastic kitchen wrap and roll out with a rolling pin, lightly dusted with flour, to make a rectangular shape of approximately 8x5". Place in the fridge to chill until nice and firm. Take the dough out of the refrigerator and, on a clean countertop roll into a 10x16" shape.

4. Place the dough with the short side facing nearest to you. Add the butter to the middle of the dough in order that the long sides are running parallel to the shorter sides.

5. Fold the lower third up to cover the butter, and brush off any extra flour. Next, fold the dough's top section down to cover and seal in the butter.

6. Take a heavy rolling pin, lightly dusted with flour, and roll out the dough to form a rectangular shape of 10x15". Fold the dough lengths into thirds, just like you would a letter. The ends of the dough that are open should be at 12 o'clock and 6 o'clock. This is the initial simple fold. Next, using kitchen wrap, cover and chill in the fridge, overnight.

7. Repeat this simple fold once more.

8. Tightly wrap the dough in plastic wrap and place the fridge for 60 minutes, to completely chill.

9. Take the dough out of the fridge and lay out on a lightly floured, clean work surface.

10. Unwrap the dough and roll it out into a rectangular shape of 10x15". Fold the top and the bottom in order that they meet in the center of the dough. Next, fold the dough into two once more, so that you achieve four layers in total.

11. Transfer the wrapped dough to the refrigerator for 2-3 hours to completely chill. Next, repeat the double fold. Make this last fold before you roll the dough out and finally cut it into your croissants.

12. To form croissant shapes, simply roll out on a clean work surface, lightly sprinkled with flour. You are aiming for a 25x15" rectangular shape with a thickness of around ?".

13. Working from the long side, fold the dough into two and with a yardstick to guide you, mark the strip that is folded into eight triangles and the dough scrapings at each end. Cut each of the double triangles into two, to make 16 individual triangles.

14. Next, using a sharp knife, make a small slit in the base of each of the triangles, and place a piece of dough trimming at the base. Start at the triangle's base and roll the dough into the shape of a log, while tucking the tip of the triangle under the body of the croissant. Bend in the two corners and form a crescent moon shape.

15. Arrange the croissants on the baking sheet and allow to literally double in size, this will take a couple of hours.

16. Around 30 minutes before finishing proofing, lightly brush each of the croissants with an egg lightly beaten with 1 tsp of cold water.

17. Preheat the main oven to 400 degrees F.

18. Place a water-filled shallow dish on the bottom shelf of the oven and bake the croissants for approximately 22-23 minutes.

19. Allow the croissants to completely cool

Savory

Chicken Bow Tie Sandwiches

Chicken salad is already delicious, but when you add pasta bow ties and serve in a flaky croissant, it's an out of this world lunch that super filling and delicious.

Portions: 4

Prep Time: 15mins

Cooking Time: N/A

Total Time: 15mins

Ingredients:

- 3 cups cooked chicken (shredded)
- 8 ounces cooked bow tie pasta
- cup scallion (chopped)
- 1 cup full-fat mayo
- 8 ounces coleslaw dressing
- Sea salt and black pepper
- 10 ounce mini pineapple chunks (drained)
- cup celery (finely chopped)
- 1 cup seedless red grapes (sliced in half)
- 1 small green apple (cored, diced)
- 4 large croissants (halved lengthwise)

Directions:

1. Toss together the shredded chicken, bow ties, and scallions.

2. In a small bowl, mix the mayo, coleslaw dressing, and add a pinch each of salt and black pepper.

3. Pour the mayo mixture over the shredded chicken mixture and stir until coated.

4. Fold in the mini pineapple chunks, chopped celery, grapes, and apple.

5. Spoon the chicken salad equally into the 4 croissants.

6. Enjoy!

Crab Mayo Salad Croissant Sandwich

Sweet crab really brings out and enhances the already buttery flavor of the croissants.

Servings: 6

Prep Time: 4mins

Cooking Time: N/A

Total Time: 4mins

Ingredients:

- 10 crab sticks (chilled, not frozen)
- ½-¾ cup mayonnaise (chilled)
- Salt
- Freshly ground black pepper
- Sugar (to taste)
- 6 fresh bakery croissants
- Iceberg lettuce (shredded)

Directions:

1. Peel the crab sticks into strips and combine with cup of mayonnaise in a bowl, mixing well to combine and adding more mayonnaise as needed.

2. Season with salt and freshly ground black pepper, and add a sprinkle of sugar to taste.

3. Slice each croissant in half and divide the shredded lettuce into 6 equal portions, and top each bottom half of croissant with the lettuce.

4. Arrange approximately 2 tablespoons of crab mayonnaise on top of the lettuce.

5. Sandwich together using the croissant top.

6. Repeat the process until all of the croissants are assembled.

7. Serve.

Cranapple Rotisserie Chicken Croissants

Looking for a yummy lunch for a crowdThese rotisserie chicken sandwiches with cranberries and apple will have family and friends begging for the recipe.

Portions: 10

Prep Time: 10mins

Cooking Time: N/A

Total Time: 10mins

Ingredients:

- 1 rotisserie chicken (shredded)
- 1 cup celery (diced)
- cup red onion (finely chopped)
- 1 red delicious apple (peeled, cored, chopped)
- 1 cup dried cranberries
- 1 cup full-fat mayo
- 10 medium whole grain croissants (halved lengthwise)
- Lettuce leaves

Directions:

1. Combine the shredded chicken, celery, red onion, chopped apple, dried cranberries, and mayo in a large bowl.

2. Spoon the mixture evenly into the 10 croissants, top each one with a few lettuce leaves and enjoy straight away.

Creamy Scrambled Egg Breakfast Croissants with Avocado

A super healthy, protein-packed breakfast to get your day off to the right start.

Servings: 1

Prep Time: 15mins

Cooking Time: 10mins

Total Time: 25mns

Ingredients:

- 2 medium eggs (scrambled)
- cup whole milk
- Salt and pepper
- 1 tsp butter
- Avocado (peeled, pitted, sliced)
- Butter lettuce leaves
- 1 large bakery croissant (split in half)

Directions:

1. First make the scrambled eggs. Beat the eggs, together with the milk, salt, and black pepper until combined.

2. Melt the butter, in a frying pan over moderate heat and when hot, add the egg mixture.

3. Once the eggs are starting to set, gently and using an inverted turner, pull the egg mixture across the frying pan to form soft curds.

4. Cook, while pulling, lifting and folding the egg mixture until no liquid egg is remaining and the mixture begins to thicken. Do not stir. Remove the pan from the heat.

5. Next, make the sandwich: Layer the avocado, along with the freshly cooked scrambled eggs, a pinch of salt, a dash of pepper and lettuce on the bottom half of the croissant.

6. Sandwich together with the croissant top and enjoy.

Croissant Baked Omelet

Yes really! Chicken and rocket stuffed croissants are cooked into a fluffy omelet for the ultimate brunch dish.

Portions: 3

Prep Time: 10mins

Cooking Time: 18mins

Total Time: 40mins

Ingredients:

- 3 medium bakery croissants (halved lengthwise)
- 3 small chicken breasts (sliced)
- Handful rocket salad
- 1 capsicum (sliced)
- 1 tbsp. full-fat plain Greek yogurt
- 2 large eggs
- 2 tbsp. whole milk
- Sea salt and black pepper
- 3 tbsp. Cheddar cheese (shredded)

Directions:

1. Preheat the main oven to 355 degrees F.

2. Stuff each croissant with an equal amount of sliced chicken, rocket salad, and capsicum.

3. Place the filled croissants in an 8" skillet and set to one side.

4. Whisk together the yogurt, egg, milk, and a pinch each of salt and black pepper in a jug.

5. Carefully pour the liquid over the croissants in the skillet. Scatter with shredded cheese.

6. Set aside for 10-12 minutes.

7. Place in the oven and bake for 15-20 minutes until set.

8. Serve hot straight from the skillet.

Croissant Croque Monsieurs

The ultimate grilled ham and cheese croissant sandwich makes a brilliant breakfast for all the family.

Servings: 4

Prep Time: 30mins

Cooking Time: 15mins

Total Time: 45mins

Ingredients:

- 1 small bunch of asparagus
- Olive oil
- Sea salt and black pepper
- 2 tbsp. salted butter
- onion (peeled, minced)
- 2 tbsp. plain flour
- 1 cup whole milk
- cup Parmesan cheese (shredded)
- Hand-squeezed juice of a small lemon
- 4 large butter croissants (halved lengthwise)
- 6 ounces deli ham (sliced)
- 8 slices Jarlsberg cheese
- Parmesan cheese (grated, to serve)

Directions:

1. First, trim the ends off the asparagus.

2. Add 1-2 tablespoons of olive oil to a frying pan over moderately high heat.

3. Add the trimmed asparagus, season well.

4. Cook for several minutes until tender with a bite. Take out of the pan and put to one side.

5. Next, make the béchamel sauce: In a pan over moderate heat, heat the butter.

6. Add the minced onion and cook for a couple of minutes, until translucent.

7. Add the flour, cook for 60 seconds more, then add the milk while slowly whisking.

8. Cook for 3 minutes, or until slightly thickened.

9. Remove from the heat and add the grated Parmesan, while stirring until incorporated. Season well with salt and black pepper and add the lemon juice.

10. Make the sandwiches by placing 2-3 ham slices on each bottom half of croissant, followed by 2 slices of cheese, and a couple spears of asparagus.

11. Place under the broiler for 2 minutes, until the cheese has melted.

12. Arrange the top halves of the croissants on top with a little of the béchamel and a scattering of Parmesan.

13. Broil on a low setting, until the cheese bubbles, for between 5-7 minutes.

14. Serve hot.

Curry Chicken Croissant Sandwiches

Great texture thanks to the walnuts and celery combine perfectly with a creamy curry sauce with a Cajun spice.

Servings: 4-6

Prep Time: 15mins

Cooking Time: N/A

Total Time: 1hour 15mins

Ingredients:

- 2cups cooked chicken breasts (finely chopped)
- cup walnuts (chopped)
- cup celery (chopped)
- 2 tbsp. onion (grated)
- cup full-fat mayo
- 2 tbsp. sour cream
- tsp curry powder
- tsp Cajun seasoning
- Lettuce leaves
- 4-6 croissants (split)

Directions:

1. Place the chicken in a large mixing bowl along with the walnuts, celery, and onion.

2. In a small mixing bowl, combine the mayo with the sour cream, curry powder, and Cajun seasoning and mix to combine thoroughly.

3. Pour the mayo mixture over the chicken mixture and stir thoroughly. Transfer to the fridge for at least 60 minutes.

4. Arrange the lettuce leaves and approximately of a cup of the chicken mixture on the top of each croissant base.

5. Sandwich together with the croissant tops.

Fig, Blue Cheese, & Prosciutto Croissant Sandwich

This sandwich is a winning combination of freshfigs, blue cheese, salty prosciutto and sweet, freshly baked croissants.

Servings: 2

Prep Time: 5mins

Cooking Time: N/A

Total Time: 5mins

Ingredients:

- pound prosciutto
- 2 bakery croissants (halved lengthwise)
- 4 ounces blue cheese (thinly sliced)
- 4 figs (sliced into thin rounds)
- cup arugula

Directions:

1. Arrange the slices of prosciutto on the bottom layer of each croissant.

2. Top with blue cheese, fig rounds, and arugula.

3. Lay the top of the croissant on top of the arugula to form a sandwich.

4. Tuck in and enjoy.

Greek Yogurt Chicken Croissant Sandwich

Fruit and nuts make for a super healthy croissant sandwich.

Servings: 4

Prep Time: 10mins

Cooking Time: N/A

Total Time: 3hours 10mins

Ingredients:

- cup plain Greek yogurt
- 1 tbsp. freshly squeezed lime juice
- tsp garlic powder
- tsp season salt
- Freshly ground black pepper
- 1 pound chicken breasts (cooked, shredded)
- cup apples (cored, finely diced)
- cup seedless grapes (halved)
- cup slivered almonds
- Lettuce
- 4 bakery croissants (split in half)

Directions:

1. In a large mixing bowl, whisk in the yogurt, freshly squeezed lime juice and garlic powder and season with salt and pepper.

2. Stir the chicken into the mixture together with the diced apples, grapes and almonds. Mix until combined and transfer to the fridge to chill for 2-3 hours.

3. Divide the lettuce between the 3 croissant bases and top with the chilled chicken mixture.

4. Add the croissant tops to form sandwiches.

Lobster Croissant Sandwich

Spoil your taste buds with this indulgent lobster croissant sandwich.

Servings: 1

Prep Time: 6mins

Cooking Time: N/A

Total Time: 6mins

Ingredients:

Celery rémoulade:

- 2 celery roots
- Freshly squeezed juice from fresh lemon
- cup mayonnaise

Sandwich:

- 1 bakery croissant (toasted)
- celery rib (finely chopped)
- 1 tsp lemon zest (grated)
- 1 tsp freshly squeezed lemon juice
- 1 tbsp. aioli
- 2 tarragon sprigs (finely chopped)
- cup celery rémoulade (recipe below)
- pound cooked lobster

Directions:

1. First, make the celery remoulade. Cut the ends off each of the celery roots and peel.

2. Using a metal cheese grater shred the celery roots over a bowl. Combine the freshly squeezed lemon juice with the mayonnaise, add to the celery roots and toss to coat.

3. To make the sandwich take a sharp knife, cut the croissant in half and toast.

4. For the sandwich: In a bowl, combine the celery, along with the lemon zest, freshly squeezed lemon juice, aioli, chopped tarragon and celery remoulade.

5. Evenly spread the mixture onto the bottom half of the croissant. Top with lobster and make a sandwich using the top half of the croissant.

Monte Cristo Sandwiches

The Monte Cristo sandwich has been around for over a century, believed to be first served in a Parisian café as a twist on the classic croque monsieur.

Portions: 4

Prep Time: 10mins

Cooking Time: 2mins

Total Time: 12mins

Ingredients:

- 4 bakery croissants (halved lengthwise)
- 2 tbsp. Dijon mustard
- pound deli ham (thinly sliced)
- 4 slices deli Swiss cheese
- Strawberry preserves
- Confectioner's sugar (for dusting)

Directions:

1. Preheat the main oven to 355 degrees F.

2. Spread each croissant bottom with Dijon mustard, and top with a of the deli ham and 1 slice of Swiss cheese.

3. Spread strawberry preserves onto each croissant top. Place the croissant tops onto the croissant bottoms and gently press down.

4. Warm each filled croissant in a microwave for 30-40 seconds.

5. Dust each croissant with confectioner's sugar before serving.

Roast Beef and Caramelized Onion Filled Croissants

Roasted beef, thinly sliced and served in a croissant with sweet caramelized onion and salty Havarti cheese, is a marriage made in heaven.

Portions: 4

Prep Time: 10mins

Cooking Time: 35mins

Total Time: 45mins

Ingredients:

- 3 tbsp. salted butter
- 4 white onions (peeled, thinly sliced)
- 2 tbsp. light brown sugar
- 4 large bakery croissants (halved lengthwise)
- 8 slices thin cut deli roasted beef
- 4 slices Havarti cheese
- 4 tomato slices
- 4 iceberg lettuce leaves

Directions:

1. Preheat your grill.

2. In a disposable baking tray, add the butter, onions, and sugar. Toss to combine and grill for approximately 35 minutes. Take out of the oven to stir at intervals. Set aside when cooked.

3. In each croissant, layer 2 slices of roasted beef, 1 slice of cheese, 1 tomato slice, 1 lettuce leaf and a of the caramelized onion.

4. Enjoy straight away.

Serrano and Manchego Croissant Sandwiches

A Spanish twist makes for a flavorsome bistro brunch, breakfast or snack.

Servings: 6

Prep Time: 30mins

Cooking Time: 17mins

Total Time: 1hour 45mins

Ingredients:

- cup semi kim milk
- 3 cups all-purpose flour
- 2 tsp active dry yeast
- cup + 2 tbsp. superfine sugar
- 5 tbsp. salted butter (softened, diced)
- Yolks from 4 medium eggs
- 6 slices manchego cheese
- 12 slices Serrano ham

Directions:

1. In a medium-sized pan, heat the milk to lukewarm.

2. To a mixing bowl, add the flour, and make a well shape in the middle, before adding the yeast along with 2 tablespoons of sugar.

3. Add the milk and stir into the flour, working from the edges of the well inwards, stir to make a thick paste-like consistency. Cover the bowl, and put to one side for 15-20 minutes.

4. Next, to the flour mixture, add the butter, followed by cup of sugar, three egg yolks, and a pinch of salt. Using your mixer's dough hook, knead into a smooth dough. Cover and put to one side for 40-45 minutes.

5. Take a baking sheet and line it with parchment paper.

6. On a lightly floured, clean work surface, roll out the dough into a 16x10" rectangular shape. Cut the dough into 6 equal portions and roll each portion up tightly from one corner to make a croissant shape.

7. Arrange the croissants on the prepared sheet, loosely cover and allow to rest at room temperature for half an hour.

8. Preheat the main oven to 400 degrees F.

9. In a mixing bowl, beat 1 egg yolk together with 2 tablespoons of cold water and lightly brush the mixture over the 6 croissants.

10. Bake in the oven for 15 minutes.

11. Remove from the oven and allow to cool on a wire baking rack.

12. Cut the croissants in half and fill each one with a slice of manchego cheese and 2 slices of Serrano ham.

Shrimp Salad with Cajun Mayo on Toasted Croissant

A tasty shrimp salad with spicy mayo on a warm, toasted croissant is the perfect breakfast or light lunch.

Servings: 4-6

Prep Time: 15mins

Cooking Time: 8mins

Total Time: 1hour 23mins

Ingredients:

- 4 cups cold water
- 1 pound medium shrimp (peeled, deveined)
- tsp Cajun seasonings
- cupred onion (peeled, minced)
- 2 tbsp. fresh parsley (chopped)
- 2tsp capers
- cup celery (minced)
- tspcayenne pepper
- cup full-fat mayo
- Juice of 1 small lemon
- Salt and black pepper (to taste)
- 4-6fresh bakery croissants
- 1 small headred lettuce (rinsed)
- 2ripe tomatoes (sliced)

Directions:

1. Add the cold water to a saucepan over high heat.

2. As soon as the water comes to a boil add the shrimp and cook for between 2-3 minutes, or until the shrimp turns pink and is tender. Drain, and transfer to a bowl and allow to cool.

3. When cool, transfer to the fridge to chill.

4. As soon as the shrimp are sufficiently cool, chop them into bite-size pieces.

5. Return the shrimp to the bowl and add the minced onion along with the chopped parsley, capers, celery, cayenne pepper, Cajun seasoning, mayo and freshly squeezed lemon juice. Mix well until incorporated.

6. Season with salt and black pepper and chill for 60 minutes.

7. When you are ready to assemble, toast the croissants in a toaster or oven for a couple of minutes, until lightly toasted and warm.

8. Using a sharp knife slice the croissants in half.

9. Arrange some red lettuce on the bottom of each croissant base and add 1-2 slices of ripe tomato.

10. Evenly spread some of the shrimp salad on top.

11. Add more lettuce and close the sandwiches, using the croissants tops.

Steak and Artichoke Croissant Sandwiches

Marinade the steak overnight for a fuller flavor and serve with artichoke hearts, crisp arugula, and sweet red onion.

Servings: 4

Prep Time: 15mins

Cooking Time: 5mins

Total Time: 8hours 20mins

Ingredients:

- 1½-2 pounds flank steaks (fat trimmed)
- 2 tsp canola oil
- 1 cup Italian dressing
- 1 cup full-fat sour cream
- 1 (14 ounce) can water-packed artichoke hearts (well drained, cut in half)
- 4 large butter croissants
- Arugula
- Red onions (finely sliced)

Directions:

1. Cut the flank steaks into strips of no more than 1½-2" wide and 3" in length.

2. In a frying pan, heat the oil, and brown the strips of steak over moderately high heat, until cooked through to your desired level of doneness.

3. Drain off any excess fat, and transfer the steak to a large bowl.

4. Pour the Italian dressing over the steak and transfer to the fridge, to chill, for 4-6 hours, or overnight.

5. The steak is ready when it has absorbed the majority of the dressing, if it has not by the time you are ready to prepare the recipe, drain off excess.

6. Next, combine the sour cream, along with the artichoke hearts, and steak strips. Mix well to combine.

7. Using a sharp knife, slice the croissants in half and evenly divide the filling between the 4 bottom halves.

8. Top with arugula and sliced red onions and close the sandwich using the remaining croissant tops.

Teriyaki Chicken Croissant

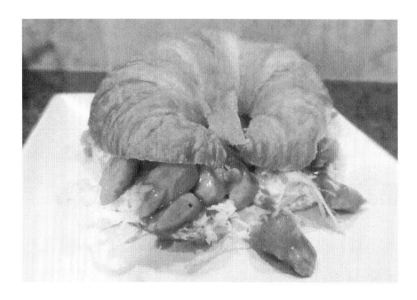

Sweet, sticky teriyaki glazed chicken served in a fresh croissant with crunchy shredded cabbage makes for snack-time heaven.

Portions: 6

Prep Time: 10mins

Cooking Time: 20mins

Total Time: 30mins

Ingredients:

- Nonstick spray
- 1pounds chicken (cubed)
- 8 ounces teriyaki glaze
- 6 tbsp. full-fat mayo
- 6 large bakery croissants
- 1cups green cabbage (shredded)

Directions:

1. Spritz a pan with nonstick spray. Add the chicken to the pan and sauté over moderately high heat until cooked. Drain away any cooking liquid.

2. Stir in the teriyaki glaze and cook for another 5-6 minutes.

3. Spread 1 tbsp. of mayo onto each croissant bottom and top each with a cup of the cabbage.

4. Divide the teriyaki chicken between the croissant bottoms. Sandwich together with the croissant tops.

5. Enjoy straight away.

Thanksgiving Turkey Salad Croissant Sandwiches

A great way to use up turkey leftovers, this deli-style sandwich is sure to become a firm family favorite.

Servings: 4

Prep Time: 10mins

Cooking Time: N/A

Total Time: 15mins

Ingredients:

- 3 cups leftover cooked turkey (diced)
- 1 stalk celery (diced small)
- 1 cup red seedless grapes (halved)
- 2 tbsp. tarragon (chopped)
- cup full-fat mayo
- cup dried cranberries
- small red onion (peeled, finely diced)
- cup caramelized pecans
- 1 (16 ounce) jar deli-sliced mild pepper rings in brine
- Salt and black pepper (to season)
- 4 bakery croissants (split in half, toasted)
- 1 (6.25 ounce) jar tomato pesto

Directions:

1. In a large mixing bowl, combine the turkey, celery, red grapes, tarragon, mayo, cranberries, red onion, and pecans. Add a splash of the brine from the pepper rings, gently stir to combine and season.

2. Spread each side of the 4 toasted croissants with tomato pesto. Evenly divide the turkey mixture between the croissant bases, top with pepper rings and serve.

Tuna Mayo Croissants

Take the classic tuna mayo sandwich to the next level by serving it in a delicious fresh croissant.

Portions: 4

Prep Time: 10mins

Cooking Time: N/A

Total Time: 10mins

Ingredients:

- 10 ounces canned tuna chunks in water (drained)
- 3 scallions (thinly sliced)
- cup dill pickles (chopped)
- 1 stalk celery (chopped)
- cup full-fat mayo
- Sea salt and black pepper
- 4 large multigrain croissants (halved lengthwise)
- 4 slices tomato
- 4 iceberg lettuce leaves
- cup banana pepper (sliced)

Directions:

1. Toss together the tuna chunks, scallions, dill pickles, and celery.

2. Stir in the mayo and a pinch each of sea salt and black pepper.

3. Spoon equal amounts of tuna mayo into each sliced croissant and top each with a slice of tomato, a lettuce leaf and a of the sliced pepper.

4. Enjoy straight away.

Turkey Avocado BLT

You just can't beat the classics, and this loaded BLT served in a buttery, flaky croissant, topped with extra deli turkey and creamy sliced avocado, is always top of our menu.

Portions: 4

Prep Time: 15mins

Cooking Time: N/A

Total Time: 15mins

Ingredients:

- 4 large buttery, flaky croissants (halved lengthwise)
- 16 ounces sliced deli turkey
- 8 rashers bacon (thick cut, cooked)
- 4 large iceberg lettuce leaves
- 1 large heirloom tomato (sliced)
- 2 small ripe avocadoes (peeled, pitted, thinly sliced)
- Sea salt and black pepper
- cup full-fat mayo

Directions:

1. To make each sandwich; on the bottom half of each croissant place 4 ounces of sliced turkey, 2 cooked bacon rashers, 1 leaf of iceberg lettuce, of the sliced tomato and avocado. Sprinkle with a little sea salt and black pepper.

2. Spread the croissant top with a of the mayo and sandwich on top.

3. Repeat to make 4 sandwiches and serve straight away.

Ultimate Breakfast Croissant

Looking for the ultimate all American weekend breakfast recipeThen search no more!

Portions: 4

Prep Time: 10mins

Cooking Time: 20mins

Total Time: 30mins

Ingredients:

- 8 rashers thick-cut bacon
- 10 medium eggs
- 2 tbsp. whole milk
- Kosher salt and black pepper
- cup Cheddar cheese (shredded)
- 4 flaky, buttery croissants (halved lengthwise)

Directions:

1. In a skillet, fry the bacon over moderately high heat until cooked and crisp, set to one side on a paper towel-lined plate. Do not discard the bacon fat.

2. Whisk the eggs together with the milk, salt, and black pepper. Pour into the pan of bacon fat and cook until scrambled and set. Sprinkle the cheese over the scrambled eggs and toss until the cheese begins to melt.

3. Stuff each croissant with 2 rashers of bacon and a of the scrambled egg.

4. Enjoy straight away!

Sweet and Savory

Almond Croissant Brunch Bake

This sweet and custardy bake is topped with crunchy flaked almonds for a scrumptious an indulgent brunch dish.

Portions: 6

Prep Time: 10mins

Cooking Time: 45mins

Total Time: 1hour 15mins

Ingredients:

- Butter (for greasing)
- 2 medium eggs
- cup granulated sugar
- 2 cups whole milk
- tsp kosher salt
- 4 large croissants (torn into pieces)
- 3 tbsp. flaked almonds

Directions:

1. Preheat the main oven to 300 degrees F. Grease a (1½-2 quart) shallow baking dish.

2. Whisk together the eggs, granulated sugar, whole milk, and kosher salt until well combined.

3. Toss the torn croissants in the liquid until coated. Set aside to soak for 7-9 minutes.

4. Transfer the mixture to the baking dish and use a spatula to smooth down the surface. Scatter with the flaked almonds.

5. Place in the oven and bake for approximately 45 minutes, until the custard has set.

6. Allow to stand for several minutes before slicing and serving.

Banana Almond Brulee Croissant Panini

A crunchy layer of brown sugar brulee makes this one sophisticated croissant panini.

Servings: 1

Prep Time: 5mins

Cooking Time: 5mins

Total Time: 10mins

Ingredients:

- 1 large bakery croissant (halved lengthwise)
- 3 tbsp. organic salted smooth almond butter
- 1 ripe large banana (peeled, sliced)
- 1 tbsp. brown sugar

Directions:

1. Preheat your panini press to a moderately high heat.

2. Spread both croissant halves with an even layer of smooth almond butter.

3. On the bottom half, arrange the banana slices.

4. Sprinkle over the brown sugar evenly and burn with a kitchen blowtorch until dark golden and bubbly.

5. Sandwich together with the croissant top.

6. Cook in the preheated press for 4-5 minutes.

7. Enjoy straight away.

Blueberry Cheesecake Croissant Bake

This croissant bake is sweet and fruity, yet sharp and tangy; just how a great cheesecake should taste.

Portions: 10

Prep Time: 10mins

Cooking Time: 40mins

Total Time: 4hours 40mins

Ingredients:

- 5cups torn croissants
- 1 cup fresh sweet blueberries
- 8 ounces full-fat cream cheese (at room temperature)
- cup granulated sugar
- 2 medium eggs
- 1 tsp vanilla essence
- 1 cup whole milk

Directions:

1. Arrange the torn croissants in an even layer in a square 9" baking pan.

2. Sprinkle with blueberries.

3. Using an electric mixer, beat together the cream cheese, granulated sugar, eggs, and vanilla essence until well combined.

4. Whisk in the milk, a little at a time, and pour the liquid over the croissants in the pan, set aside to soak for 3-4 hours.

5. Preheat the main oven to 350 degrees F.

6. Place the baking pan in the oven and bake for just over 35 minutes*, until set.

7. Serve warm.

*If the top is browning too quickly, cover with aluminum foil for the final 10 minutes of baking.

Campfire Croissants

Enjoy this campfire classic in a new and fun way, swapping dry graham crackers for buttery and soft flaky croissants.

Portions: 6

Prep Time: 10mins

Cooking Time: 5mins

Total Time: 15mins

Ingredients:

- 2 tsp brown sugar
- tsp cinnamon
- tsp nutmeg
- 4 tbsp. salted butter (melted)
- 6 large croissants (halved lengthwise)
- 18 large marshmallows
- 6 ounces semisweet chocolate squares

Directions:

1. Preheat your grill for direct grilling on a moderately high heat.

2. Combine the sugar, cinnamon, and nutmeg in a small dish.

3. Brush each croissant half with melted butter on the cut-sides only. Sprinkle each croissant half with the spiced sugar.

4. Take 6 skewers and slide 3 marshmallows onto each.

5. Toast each croissant half, buttered side down, for 60 seconds. Take off the grill and divide the chocolate squares equally among the bottom halves.

6. Grill the marshmallows for 90 seconds, turning once. Slide 3 marshmallows onto each chocolatey croissant base.

7. Sandwich together with the toasted croissant tops.

8. Enjoy straight away!

Chickpea and Fruit Salad Croissant Sandwiches

These packed croissant sandwiches are full of nutritious goodies including protein-packed chickpeas, roasted sunflower seeds, strawberries, honey crisp apple, and aromatic fresh basil.

Portions: 4

Prep Time: 10mins

Cooking Time: N/A

Total Time: 10mins

Ingredients:

- 15 ounces canned chickpeas (drained, rinsed)
- cup full-fat mayo
- 1tsp Dijon mustard
- 1 tsp American mustard
- tsp sea salt
- Pinch black pepper
- cup fresh strawberries (hulled, chopped)
- 2 celery stalks (chopped)
- cup honey crisp apple (chopped)
- 2 tbsp. sunflower seeds (roasted)
- 3tbsp. fresh basil (chopped)
- 4 multigrain croissants (sliced lengthwise)

Directions:

1. Mash the chickpeas in a large bowl. Set aside for a moment.

2. Mix the mayo, mustards, salt, and pepper. Stir the mixture into the mashed chickpeas until combined.

3. Fold in the strawberries, celery, apple, sunflower seeds, and chopped basil, until incorporated.

4. Spoon the chickpea salad equally into the 4 croissants and serve.

Chocolate Croissant Bread Pudding

A modern take on a classic bread pudding; this chocolatey creation wins hands down!

Portions: 12

Prep Time: 15mins

Cooking Time: 1hour

Total Time: 1hour 45mins

Ingredients:

- Nonstick spray
- 6 large bakery croissants*
- cup semisweet choc chips
- 8 medium eggs
- 5 cups skim milk
- 1 cup granulated sugar
- 1tsp vanilla essence

Directions:

1. Preheat the main oven to 350 degrees F. Spritz a large, rectangular baking dish with nonstick spray.

2. Arrange the croissant bottoms in the dish. Scatter with choc chips and replace the croissant tops.

3. In a jug, whisk together the eggs, skim milk, granulated sugar, and vanilla essence and pour over the croissants in the dish. Set aside to soak for several minutes.

4. Place in the oven and bake for approximately an hour.

5. Allow to stand for 10-15 minutes before slicing and serving.

*Preferably one day old.

Cinnamon Toffee Croissant Pudding

Cinnamon toffee makes for a rich and decadent pudding that provides the ultimate in comfort food.

Portions: 12

Prep Time: 15mins

Cooking Time: 35mins

Total Time: 1hour 10mins

Ingredients:

Pudding:

- 3 medium eggs (lightly beaten)
- 4 cups skim milk
- 2 cups granulated sugar
- 4 tsp almond essence
- 3 tsp cinnamon
- tsp nutmeg
- 10 bakery croissants (torn into large pieces)
- 1 cup toffee chips
- 1 cup toasted pecans (chopped)
- 1 cup milk choc chips
- Butter (for greasing)

Sauce:

- 1 cup granulated sugar
- cup half & half
- cup salted butter (chilled, cubed)
- tsp vanilla essence

Directions:

1. In a large bowl, whisk together the eggs, skim milk, granulated sugar, almond essence, cinnamon, and nutmeg. Gently stir the torn croissants into the liquid.

2. Fold in the toffee chips, chopped nuts, and choc chips. Set aside for 15-20 minutes.

3. Preheat the main oven to 350 degrees F. Grease a large rectangular baking dish.

4. Pour the pudding mixture into the baking dish.

5. Bake for just over half an hour until set.

6. Prepare the sauce. In a small saucepan, bring to boil the sugar, half & half, and butter until melted. Turn the heat down to a simmer and cook for 5-6 minutes. Take off the heat and stir in the vanilla essence.

7. Serve the hot sauce with the warm puddings.

Cranberry and Walnut Cream Cheese Croissant Sandwiches

Enjoy this campfire classic in a new and fun way, swapping dry graham crackers for buttery and soft flaky croissants.

Portions: 6

Prep Time: 10mins

Cooking Time: N/A

Total Time: 10mins

Ingredients:

- 4 ounces full-fat cream cheese
- 4 tbsp. cranberry sauce
- Pinch cinnamon
- 2tbsp. walnuts (finely chopped)
- 1 wholegrain bakery croissant (halved lengthwise)
- Thinly sliced green apple
- 1 tbsp. organic honey

Directions:

1. In a bowl, beat together the cream cheese and cranberry sauce until combined.

2. Stir in the cinnamon and fold in the chopped walnuts until incorporated.

3. Spoon a generous amount of the cream cheese mixture onto the bottom of each croissant half.

4. Top with sliced green apple and drizzle over a little honey and sandwich together with the croissant tops.

5. Serve straight away!

Fruity Dessert Croissant Casserole

This croissant casserole is a super simple and quick dessert that doesn't compromise on flavor; the perfect midweek treat.

Portions: 6

Prep Time: 10mins

Cooking Time: 20mins

Total Time: 40mins

Ingredients:

- 4 large croissants (torn into pieces)
- 4 large strawberries (hulled, halved)
- 1 cup fresh blueberries
- 1 medium egg
- cup granulated sugar
- tsp ground cinnamon
- Pinch kosher salt
- cup whole milk
- cup freshly squeezed orange juice
- tsp vanilla essence

Directions:

1. Preheat your main oven to 350 degrees F.

2. Place the torn croissants in the base of a casserole dish.

3. Scatter with sliced strawberries and blueberries.

4. In a jug, whisk together the egg, sugar, cinnamon, salt, whole milk, orange juice, and vanilla until combined.

5. Pour the liquid over the croissants and set aside for several minutes to soak.

6. Place in the oven and bake for 10 minutes, remove and cover with aluminum foil, bake for a final 10 minutes.

7. Allow to cool a little before slicing and serving warm.

Gruyere and Peach Croissants with Sweet Mustard

Sweet peaches combine with mustard and nutty tasting cheese for an amazing sweet 'n savory snack.

Portions: 3

Prep Time: 10mins

Cooking Time: 5mins

Total Time: 15mins

Ingredients:

- 1 tbsp. wholegrain mustard
- 1tsp good quality balsamic vinegar
- 1 tbsp. virgin olive oil
- Salt and black pepper
- 6 mini bakery croissants (sliced lengthwise)
- 6 slices gruyere cheese
- 1 ripe medium peach (pitted, thinly sliced)

Directions:

1. Preheat the broiler.

2. In a bowl, whisk together the wholegrain mustard, balsamic vinegar, oil, salt, and black pepper. Set to one side.

3. Toast the croissant halves.

4. Place 1 slice of gruyere on each croissant base and heat under the broiler until the cheese melts.

5. Arrange a few slices of peach on top. Drizzle with dressing and sandwich together with the toasted croissant tops.

Hazelnut Chocolate and Strawberry Croissant French Toast

Fresh juicy strawberries prevent this indulgent hazelnut and chocolate croissant French toast from being too heavy and rich, meaning you return, guilt-free for seconds!

Portions: 6

Prep Time: 15mins

Cooking Time: 35mins

Total Time: 5hours 50mins

Ingredients:

- Butter (for greasing)
- 8 ounces full-fat cream cheese
- cup hazelnut chocolate spread
- 8 large bakery-style croissants (halved lengthwise)
- 4 medium eggs
- 1 cup whole milk
- 1 tsp vanilla essence
- cup salted butter (melted)
- cup + 1 tbsp. granulated sugar
- 1 tbsp. sweetened cocoa powder
- cup fresh strawberries (hulled, sliced)

Directions:

1. Grease a baking dish.

2. In a mixing bowl, beat together the cream cheese and hazelnut chocolate spread until combined. Spread 4 tbsp. of the mixture onto the 8 croissant bases. Sandwich together with the 8 croissant tops. Slice each croissant in half to make 16 mini croissant sandwiches. Arrange in the baking dish.

3. In a jug whisk together the eggs, whole milk, vanilla essence, melted butter, cup of granulated sugar, and cocoa powder.

4. Pour the liquid over the croissants in the dish. Cover with foil and chill for 4-5 hours*.

5. Preheat the main oven to 350 degrees F.

6. Baste the croissants with any liquid pooling in the dish before placing in the oven for approximately 35 minutes, or until set.

7. Toss the strawberries in the remaining granulated sugar before scattering over the warm French toast.

8. Slice and serve warm.

*Or overnight if you intend to enjoy this dish for breakfast.

Maple Bacon and Sausage Croissant Squares

We can't think of a better way to enjoy our bacon and sausage in the morning than in a creamy bake dripping with maple syrup.

Portions: 8-10

Prep Time: 15mins

Cooking Time: 1hour 10mins

Total Time: 1hour 55mins

Ingredients:

- Butter (for greasing)
- 6 large croissants (sliced open lengthwise)
- 12 rashers bacon (cooked)
- 9 sausages (cooked, halved lengthwise)
- 10 medium eggs
- 1cups whole milk
- cup heavy cream
- 2 tsp kosher salt
- 1 tsp black pepper
- Maple syrup (for serving)

Directions:

1. Preheat the main oven to 350 degrees F. Grease a large casserole dish.

2. In each croissant, place 2 bacon rashers, and 3 halves of sausage. Arrange the filled croissants in a large casserole dish.

3. In a mixing bowl, beat together the eggs, whole milk, cream, kosher salt, and black pepper, until combined.

4. Pour the liquid over the croissants in the dish. Cover with a piece of parchment and press down. Place a heavy dish on top of the paper to weigh down. Transfer to the fridge to chill for half an hour.

5. Remove the heavy dish and parchment. Cover the casserole dish with aluminum foil and place in the oven.

6. Bake for 40 minutes, before discarding the aluminum foil and baking for a final half an hour.

7. Allow to cool a little before slicing into squares and serving warm with a drizzle of maple syrup.

Pumpkin Pie Baked Croissants

Give plain and boring croissants a festive makeover by stuffing them with pumpkin pie filling and baking them until warm and fragrant.

Portions: 6

Prep Time: 10mins

Cooking Time: 20mins

Total Time: 35mins

Ingredients:

- cup unsalted butter (at room temperature)
- cup granulated sugar
- cup pureed pumpkin
- 1 egg
- 1 tbsp. all-purpose flour
- tsp vanilla essence
- tsp pumpkin pie spice
- Pinch kosher salt
- 6 large bakery croissants (halved lengthwise)
- Confectioner's sugar (for dusting)

Directions:

1. Preheat the main oven to 350 degrees F. Line a baking sheet with parchment.

2. Beat together the butter and granulated sugar until fluffy.

3. Beat in the pureed pumpkin, egg, all-purpose flour, vanilla essence, pie spice, and kosher salt for 2-3 minutes until super light.

4. Spread 1-2 tbsp. of the mixture into each sliced croissant.

5. Arrange the filled croissants on a baking sheet. Spread any remaining pumpkin mixture on top of the croissants.

6. Place in the oven and bake for 20 minutes.

7. Allow to cool a little before dusting with confectioner's sugar and serving warm.

Strawberry and Basil Crispy Prosciutto Croissant Sandwiches

These fully loaded croissant sandwiches are full to bursting with melted Brie, crispy prosciutto, creamy avocado, sweet strawberries, runny fried eggs, herby basil and are finished off with a drizzle of organic honey!

Portions: 2

Prep Time: 10mins

Cooking Time: 10mins

Total Time: 20mins

Ingredients:

- 2 large croissants (halved lengthwise)
- 5 ounces Brie cheese (sliced)
- 4 thin slices prosciutto
- 1 ripe medium avocado (peeled, pitted, sliced)
- 4 large sweet strawberries (hulled, sliced)
- 2 fried eggs
- Salt and black pepper
- 6 fresh basil leaves
- Organic honey

Directions:

1. Preheat the main oven to 450 degrees F.

2. Arrange the bottom halves of the croissants on a baking sheet. Top each with an equal amount of sliced Brie.

3. In the remaining space on the baking sheet, arrange the sliced prosciutto.

4. Bake in the oven for 8-10 minutes, until the prosciutto is crispy and the Brie is beginning to melt.

5. Top each cheesy croissant half with two slices of prosciutto, half of the sliced avocado and strawberries, one fried egg, a pinch each of salt and pepper and a few basil leaves. Drizzle with a little honey and sandwich together with the croissant tops.

6. Enjoy immediately.

Tropical Fruit and Honeyed Cream Cheese Croissant Sandwich

Why go for calorie-laden cakes or muffins when you can indulge in a fruit packed, creamy croissant treat?

Portions: 1

Prep Time: 10mins

Cooking Time: N/A

Total Time: 10mins

Ingredients:

- 2 tbsp. full-fat cream cheese (at room temperature)
- 2 tsp organic honey
- Pinch cinnamon
- 1 large croissant (halved lengthwise)
- 1 tbsp. toasted slivered almonds
- cup raspberries
- cup banana (sliced)
- cup ripe mango (chopped)

Directions:

1. In a mixing bowl, beat together the cream cheese, honey, and cinnamon until combined.

2. Spread both croissant halves with the honeyed cream cheese and scatter with toasted almonds. Arrange the fruit on the bottom half of the croissant.

3. Take the croissant top and form a sandwich.

4. Enjoy!

Author's Afterthoughts

Thanks ever so much to each of my cherished readers for investing the time to read this book!

I know you could have picked from many other books but you chose this one. So a big thanks for downloading this book and reading all the way to the end.

If you enjoyed this book or received value from it, I'd like to ask you for a favor. Please take a few minutes to post an honest and heartfelt review on Amazon.com. Your support does make a difference and helps to benefit other people.

Thanks!

Daniel Humphreys

About the Author

Daniel Humphreys

Many people will ask me if I am German or Norman, and my answer is that I am 100% unique! Joking aside, I owe my cooking influence mainly to my mother who was British! I can certainly make a mean Sheppard's pie, but when it comes to preparing Bratwurst sausages and drinking beer with friends, I am also all in!

I am taking you on this culinary journey with me and hope you can appreciate my diversified background. In my 15 years career as a chef, I never had a dish returned to me by one of clients, so that should say something about me! Actually, I will take that back. My worst critic is my four years old son, who refuses to taste anything that is green color. That shall pass, I am sure.

My hope is to help my children discover the joy of cooking and sharing their creations with their loved ones, like I did all my life. When you develop a passion for cooking and my suspicious is that you have one as well, it usually sticks for life. The best advice I can give anyone as a professional chef is invest. Invest your time, your heart in each meal you are creating. Invest also a little money in good cooking hardware and quality ingredients. But most of all enjoy every meal you prepare with YOUR friends and family!

Printed in Great Britain
by Amazon

28271831R00074